Pledge of Allegiance

Written by Douglas M. Rife
Illustrated by Bron Smith

Teaching & Learning Company
1204 Buchanan St., P.O. Box 10
Carthage, IL 62321-0010

This book belongs to

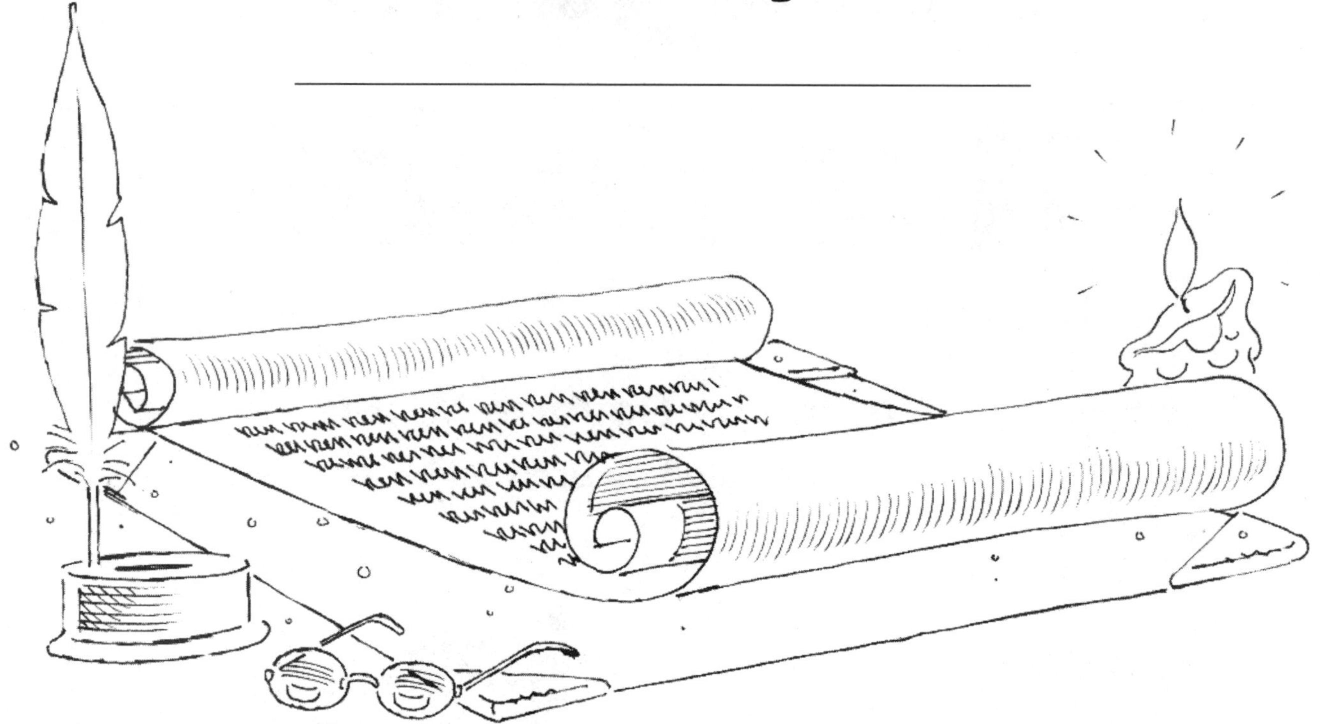

Cover photo by Images and More Photography

ISBN No. 1-57310-128-1

Printing No. 987654321

Teaching & Learning Company
1204 Buchanan St., P.O. Box 10
Carthage, IL 62321-0010

Table of Contents

Dear Teacher or Parent,

We live in a world where symbols convey meaning in an instant. Five-year-olds know that the golden arches represent McDonald's®. Adults recognize the donkey and the elephant as the symbols for the Democratic and Republican Parties. And most of us remember that the cracked bell in front of Independence Hall symbolizes liberty. But few symbols stir emotions of national pride and patriotism in us the way the United States flag does. Justice John Paul Stevens wrote this about our flag: "It is more than a proud symbol of the courage, the determination, and the gifts of nature that transform thirteen fledgling Colonies into a world power. It is a symbol of freedom, of equal opportunity, of religious tolerance, and of good will for other peoples who share our aspirations. The symbol carries its message to dissidents both at home and abroad who may have no interest at all in our national unity or survival. The value of the flag as a symbol cannot be measured."

The purpose of this book is to provide a brief history of the United States flag and of the Pledge of Allegiance that honors it and our country. Students have held their hands over their hearts and recited a pledge of one kind or another in classrooms across America since the late 1800s. The study of the flag and the pledge is a good point at which to begin discussions about what it means to be a good citizen, what it means to be an American and what the flag means as a national symbol.

No book of activities about the United States flag and the Pledge of Allegiance would be complete without including opposing viewpoints, for dissent is truly American. The study of a flag burning case and a Supreme Court decision about the Pledge of Allegiance require students to think about issues central to the Constitution itself.

Sincerely,

Douglas

Douglas M. Rife

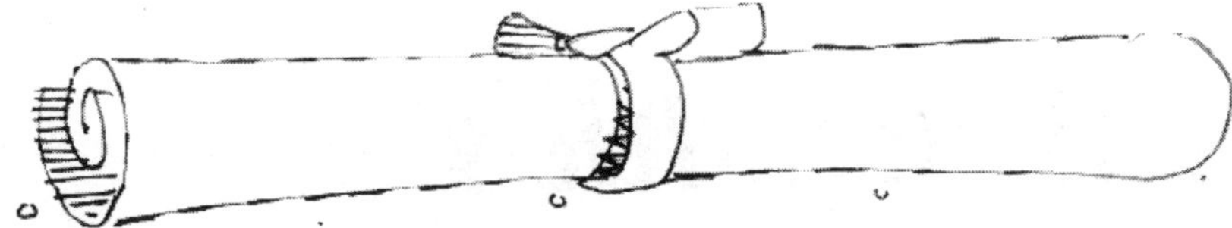

Objectives

After completing the following activities	the students should be able to . . .
The History of the Flag of the United States	1. identify the parts of a flag 2. explain the history of the United States flag
The Pledge of Allegiance	1. understand the history of the Pledge of Allegiance 2. explain the meaning of the Pledge of Allegiance 3. compare the United States' pledge to the pledge of allegiance to the Guyana flag
Political Cartoons	1. define symbols 2. identify the political figures 3. interpret the political message of the cartoonist 4. draw own cartoons 5. understand the flag as speech
The Supreme Court and the Pledge of Allegiance	1. read and explain Supreme Court decisions 2. evaluate the decision 3. form opinions about those decisions 4. understand the appeals process 5. explain freedom of expression 6. synthesize both sides of the "Symbolic Speech" issue

How to Use These Activities

The text and activities in this book are written to be used with students at various skill levels. As the book progresses, the activities become more complex, requiring students to use higher levels of thinking. The book is divided into the following four sections:

The History of the United States Flag

No other symbol of the United States is as revered as the United States flag and few are as old. Like many of our institutions, the founders of our country borrowed from England to build the foundations of the new government–that was true of the flag as well. Our flag had its origins in the Union Jack, our first flag contained the Union Jack in its canton. This section explains the beginnings of flags as a national symbol and describes notable flags in U.S. history. Distribute *The History of the Flag* handouts. Use the *Flag Match* and *Parts of the Flag* activities to test comprehension.

The History of the Pledge of Allegiance

The Pledge of Allegiance is, of course, inextricably linked to the United States flag. The history of the pledge is just a little over a century old and got its beginnings from a small part of an article written to celebrate Columbus' 400th anniversary of his famous landing. The activities in this section, The Vocabulary Builder and Pledge Crossword, were developed to help students gain a better understanding of what the words in the pledge actually mean. The third activity in this section allows students to compare our flag and pledge with Guyana's. Comparisons allow students to view items common to them in a clear way.

Political Cartoons and the Flag Burning Controversy

In 1984, a political protester burned an American flag. The protester was convicted under Texas law for desecration of the flag. The conviction was overturned in a 5-4 Supreme Court decision in 1989. The decision instantly became grist for politicians, editorialists and political cartoonists. We have included two cartoons that portray differing viewpoints about the decision. These cartoons can be handed to students individually or used with the whole classroom as a discussion starter. This section of the book focuses on freedom of speech and what constitutes speech and the ongoing debate surrounding symbolic speech. The cartoon quiz activity can be used to spark class discussions or as a comprehension test.

The Supreme Court and the Pledge of Allegiance

The flag, the pledge and symbolic speech are all tied together. In this section, students are introduced to two Supreme Court cases–1940 and 1943–that dealt with students who refused to recite the pledge or salute the flag because of religious convictions. Text from the court decisions explains why the Supreme Court ruled as it did in both cases. The "Understanding" activities after each section can be used as posttests to check comprehension or used to spark classroom discussion.

The History of Flags and What They Mean

The use of flags dates as far back as 1122 BC in China. Emperor Chou had a white flag carried in front of him. The navy of Athens flew a purple flag as early as fifth century BC. These early flags were generally used as battle insignia or as a personal sign of the commander or the king for whom the soldiers were battling. Royal standards were carried into battle or displayed outside a castle as a way of making it known that the king was, in fact, in residence. The same was true if the monarch was present on a ship. For the most part, flags were used as a symbol of personal authority of kings and commanders. Flags were used to identify the soldiers in battle. At first, an insignia was worn on the fronts and backs of soldiers' armor. Flags did not become symbols of nations until centuries later.

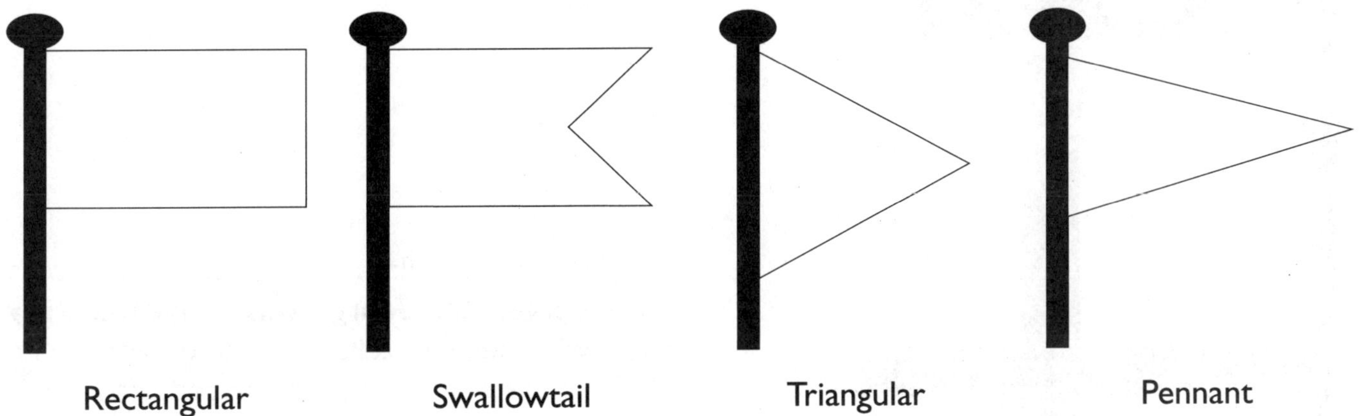

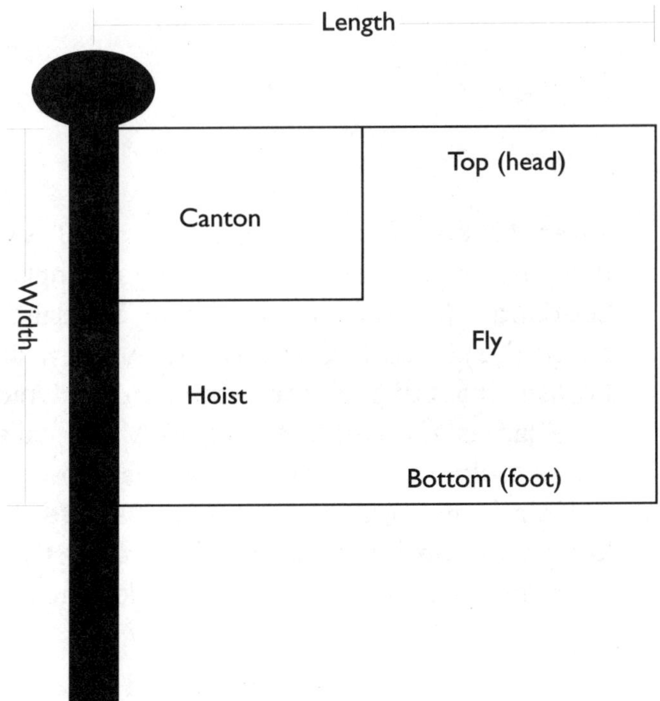

Henry Ward Beecher said, "A thoughtful mind when it sees a nation's flag, sees not the flag only, but the nation itself, and whatever may be its symbols, its insignia, he reads chiefly in the flag the government, the principles, the truths, the history, which belong to the nation that sets forth." Beecher's description of the flag is what flags have become today.

Though flags were symbols of kings and queens, and now nations, the word *flag* originated from the Saxon word *fflaken*, which means "to fly or float in the wind."

The History of the Flag of the United States

According to Scottish legend, King Malcolm I took the Cross of St. Andrew (Scotland's patron saint) as a national flag because he saw the cross in a vision in the clear blue sky the day before the battle of Brunanbaugh in 937. This type of an X-shaped cross is referred to as a saltire.

One of the earliest flags of England is the Cross of St. George. St. George was a third century martyr who, legend tells, slew a dragon. The English armies began wearing the red cross on a white background as early as 1277, when Edward I had his armies wear the insignia into battle.

After Queen Elizabeth died in 1603 with no heirs, her cousin became the king of England and Scotland. In 1606, England and Scotland combined the Scottish Cross of St. Andrew and the English Cross of St. George to form the Union flag. King James merged the two in a flag called the King's Colours. At first this flag was flown on the jack-staff of royal and navy ships and became known as the Union Jack. Over time the King's Colours became known as the Union Jack.

Sometimes called the Cambridge Flag, this flag combines the Union Jack of Great Britain with the stripes. It shows our British heritage and the stripes that represent the original 13 colonies. General George Washington raised this flag in January of 1776 at Cambridge, Massachusetts.

On June 14, 1777, the Continental Congress passed a resolution declaring "that the flag of the thirteen United States be thirteen stripes alternating red and white; that the union be thirteen stars, white in a blue field, representing a new constellation." The stars in the field represent only one arrangement that was popular during the revolution. Five-pointed stars are called mullets.

This flag design was famous because of the colonial battle victory at Bennington, Vermont, that kept a British raiding party from capturing a military storehouse. The skirmish took place on August 16, 1777. John Stark said to his men that night, "My men, yonder are the Hessians. They were bought for Seven pounds and ten pence a man. Are you worth more? Prove it. Tonight, the American flag floats from yonder hill or Molly Stark sleeps a widow!" Notice the six-pointed stars on this flag. These stars are called estoile.

Vermont and Kentucky were the first two states added to the Union after the original 13. When they were admitted not only were two stars added to the flag, but also two stripes. This was the flag that was the inspiration for Francis Scott Key who wrote "The Star-Spangled Banner" from a British ship. Key watched as the British bombarded Fort McHenry, Baltimore, Maryland, the night of September 13, 1814. This was the flag of the United States from 1795 until 1818.

On April 4, 1818, Congress passed a law returning to the tradition of the United States' flag with 13 stripes. Congress realized that adding a stripe with each additional state would soon make the flag an unusual shape. So, Congress provided for a new star to be added for each new state admitted to the Union.

This flag of 1818, known as the Great Star Flag, shows the creativity of design that was used by some flag makers. In this flag, the 20 stars form a large star.

During the Civil War, a defiant Abraham Lincoln would not allow the stars representing the southern states to be removed from the flag.

Name ________________________________

Flag Match

Match the flags below.

a. Flag of St. Andrew
b. Flag of St. George
c. Union Jack
d. Grand Union Flag (1776)
e. Stars and Stripes (1777)
f. Bennington Flag (1777)
g. The Star-Spangled Banner (1795)
h. Great Star Flag (1818)

______ 1.

______ 2.

______ 3.

______ 4.

______ 5.

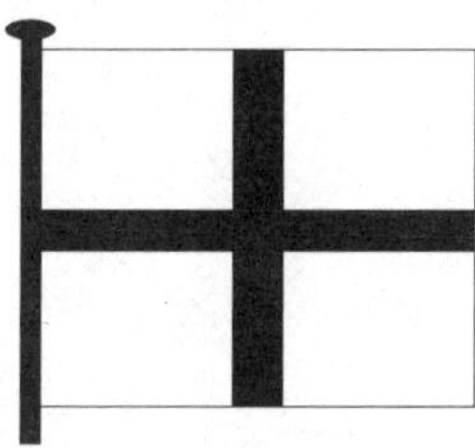

______ 6.

______ 7.

______ 8.

Beyond the Flag Match

Study the Union Jack from the Revolutionary War period, and compare it to Britain's flag today. How are the two flags different?

Bonus

Why are the flags different?

Name ______________________________

Parts of the Flag

Match the parts of the flag.

a. top
b. bottom
c. hoist
d. length
e. canton
f. width
g. fly

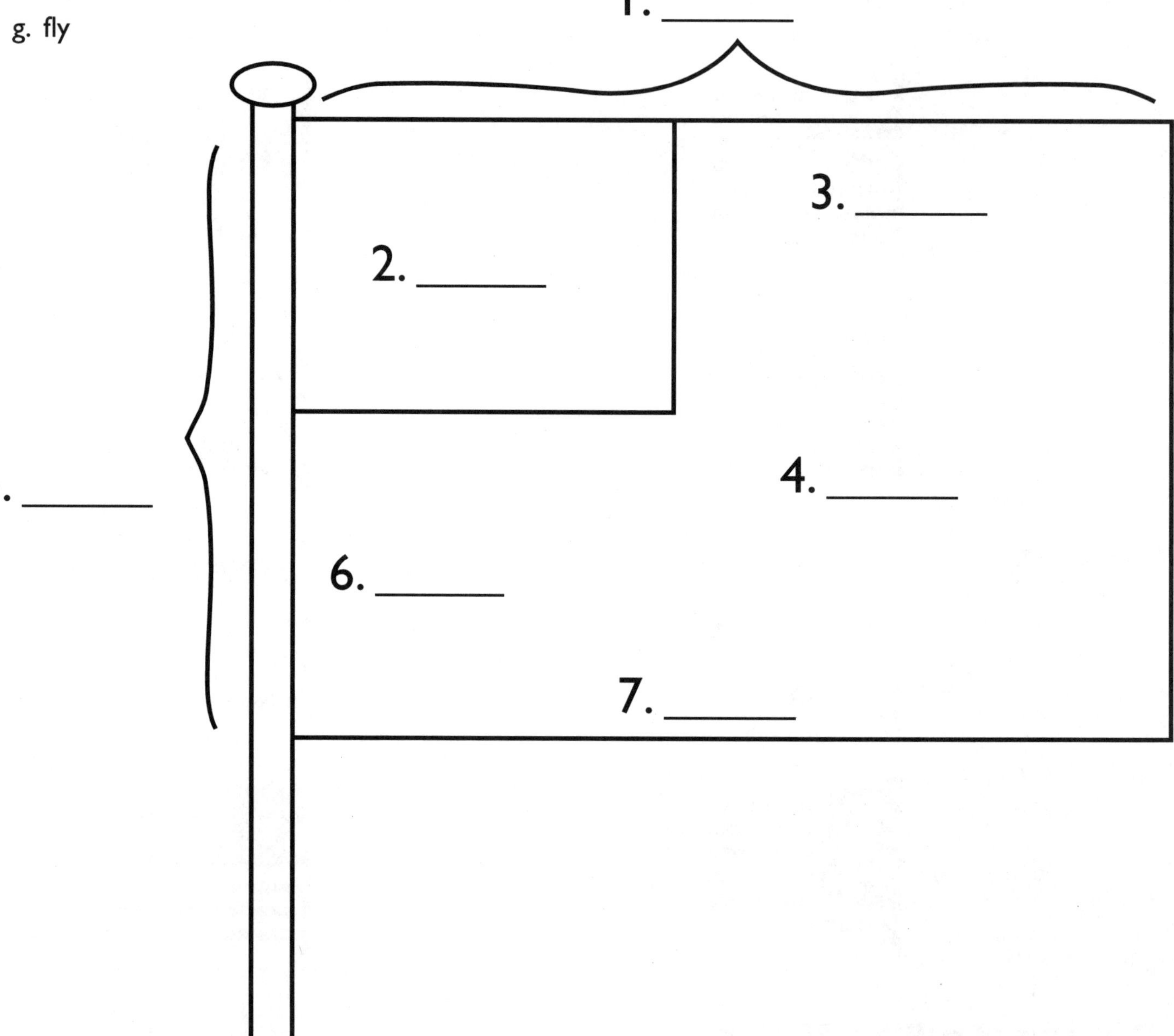

Beyond the Parts of the Flag

Using your knowledge of the history of the United States flag, design a new flag to represent the United States on the back of this sheet. Be prepared to explain what the colors and symbols in your flag mean.

The Pledge of Allegiance
The Youth's Companion

446 THE YOUTH'S COMPANION. SEPTEMBER 8, 1892.

National School Celebration of Columbus Day.

THE OFFICIAL PROGRAMME.

Let every pupil and friend of the Schools who reads THE COMPANION, at once present personally the following programme to the Teachers, Superintendents, School Boards, and Newspapers in the towns and cities in which they reside. Not one School in America should be left out in this Celebration.

IN obedience to an Act of Congress, the President on July 21 issued a Proclamation recommending that October 21, the 400th Anniversary of the Discovery of America, be celebrated everywhere in America by suitable exercises in the schools.

A uniform Programme for every school in America, to be used on Columbus Day, simultaneously with the dedicatory exercises of the World's Columbian Exposition grounds in Chicago, will give an impressive unity to the popular celebration. Accordingly, when the Superintendents of Education, last February, accepted THE COMPANION'S plan for this national Public School celebration, they instructed their Executive Committee to prepare an Official Programme of exercises for the Day, uniform for every school.

To enable preparations for the National School Celebration in every community to begin *immediately*, this Executive Committee now publish through THE COMPANION

THE OFFICIAL PROGRAMME

for the National Columbian Public School Celebration

Of October 21, 1892.

NOTE.—*The instructions for the proper conduct of these exercises are given in the small type, the successive exercises themselves in the large type.*

The schools should assemble at 9 A. M. in their various rooms. At 9.30 the detail of Veterans is expected to arrive. It is to be met at the entrance of the yard by the Color-Guard of pupils, escorted with dignity to the building, and presented to the Principal. The Principal then gives the signal, and the several teachers conduct their pupils to the yard, to beat of drum or other music, and arrange them in a hollow square about the flag, the Veterans and Color-Guard taking places by the flag itself. The Master of Ceremonies then gives the command "Attention!" and begins the exercises by reading the Proclamation.

1. READING OF THE PRESIDENT'S PROCLAMATION, *by the Master of Ceremonies.*

At the close of the reading he announces: "In accordance with this recommendation by the President of the United States, and as a sign of our devotion to our country, let the Flag of the Nation be unfurled above this School."

2. RAISING OF THE FLAG, *by the Veterans.*

As the Flag reaches the top of the staff, the Veterans will lead the assemblage in "Three Cheers for 'Old Glory.'"

3. SALUTE TO THE FLAG, *by the Pupils.*

At a signal from the Principal the pupils, in ordered ranks, hands to the side, face the Flag. Another signal is given; every pupil gives the Flag the military salute—right hand lifted, palm downward, to a line with the forehead and close to it. Standing thus, all repeat together, slowly: "I pledge allegiance to my Flag and the Republic for which it stands: one Nation indivisible, with Liberty and Justice for all." At the words, "to my Flag," the right hand is extended gracefully, palm upward, towards the Flag, and remains in this gesture till the end of the affirmation; whereupon all hands immediately drop to the side. Then, still standing, as the instruments strike a chord, all will sing AMERICA—"My Country, 'tis of Thee."

4. ACKNOWLEDGMENT OF GOD. Prayer or Scripture.

5. SONG OF COLUMBUS DAY, *by Pupils and Audience.*

Contributed by The Youth's Companion.

Air: Lyons.

Columbia, my land! all hail the glad day
When first to thy strand Hope pointed the way:
Hail him who thro' darkness first followed the Flame
That led where the Mayflower of Liberty came.

Dear Country, the star of the valiant and free!
Thy exiles afar are dreaming of thee.
No fields of the Earth so enchantingly shine,
No air breathes such incense, such music as thine.

Humanity's home! thy sheltering breast
Gives welcome and room to strangers oppress'd.
Pale children of Hunger and Hatred and Wrong
Find life in thy freedom and joy in thy song.

Thy fairest estate the lowly may hold,
Thy poor may grow great, thy feeble grow bold
For worth is the watchword to noble degree,
And manhood is mighty where manhood is free.

O Union of States, and union of souls!
Thy promise awaits, thy future unfolds,
And earth from her twilight is hailing the sun,
That rises where people and rulers are one.

THERON BROWN.

6. THE ADDRESS, "The Meaning of the Four Centuries."

A Declamation of the Special Address prepared for the occasion by THE YOUTH'S COMPANION.

7. THE ODE, "Columbia's Banner."

A Reading of the Poem written for the occasion by Edna Dean Proctor.

Here should follow whatever additional Exercises, Patriotic Recitations, Historic Representations, or Chorals may be desired.

8. ADDRESSES BY CITIZENS, and National Songs.

EXECUTIVE COMMITTEE.

FRANCIS BELLAMY, *Chairman, representing The Youth's Companion,* Boston, Mass.
JOHN W. DICKINSON, Secretary of the Massachusetts Board of Education.
THOMAS B. STOCKWELL, Commissioner of Rhode Island Public Schools.
W. R. GARRETT, Superintendent of Public Instruction of Tennessee.
W. C. HEWITT, Superintendent of Michigan Educational Exhibit at World's Fair.

SPECIAL NOTICE.—*This Official Programme, printed on a four-page sheet, including the songs and the President's Proclamation, will be supplied by "The Youth's Companion" at $1.00 per hundred. The songs entire should be in the hands of all the audience. With every order will be sent single copies of the Ode and the Address; also a four-page sheet containing suggestions on "How to Observe Columbus Day." An abbreviated and simplified form of the Address will be supplied for Primary Schools.*

IT has been a pleasure to THE COMPANION to contribute, as its special gift, the Original Poems and the Address which are to be rendered on the occasion.

Contributed by The Youth's Companion.

THE ODE FOR COLUMBUS DAY.

"COLUMBIA'S BANNER."

"God helping me," cried Columbus, "though fair or foul the breeze,
I will sail and sail till I find the land beyond the western seas!"—
So an eagle might leave its eyrie, bent, though the blue should bar,
To fold its wings on the loftiest peak of an undiscovered star!
And into the vast and void abyss he followed the setting sun;
Nor gulfs nor gales could fright his sails till the wondrous quest was done.
But O the weary vigils, the murmuring, torturing days,
Till the Pinta's gun, and the shout of "Land!" set the black night ablaze!
Till the shore lay fair as Paradise in morning's balm and gold,
And a world was won from the conquered deep, and the tale of the ages told!

Uplift the starry Banner! The best age is begun!
We are the heirs of the mariners whose voyage that morn was done.
Measureless lands Columbus gave and rivers through zones that roll,
But his rarest, noblest bounty was a New World for the Soul!
For he sailed from the Past with its stifling walls, to the Future's open sky,
And the ghosts of gloom and fear were laid as the breath of heaven went by;
And the pedant's pride and the lordling's scorn were lost, in that vital air,
As fogs are lost when sun and wind sweep ocean blue and bare;
And Freedom and larger Knowledge dawned clear, the sky to span,
The birthright, not of priest or king, but of every child of man!

Uplift the New World's Banner to greet the exultant sun!
Let its rosy gleams still follow his beams as swift to west they run,
Till the wide air rings with shout and hymn to welcome it shining high,
And our eagle from lone Katahdin to Shasta's snow can fly
In the light of its stars as fold on fold is flung to the autumn sky!
Uplift it, Youths and Maidens, with songs and loving cheers;
Through triumphs, raptures, it has waved, through agonies and tears.

Columbia looks from sea to sea and thrills with joy to know
Her myriad sons, as one, would leap to shield it from a foe!
And you who soon will be the State, and shape each great decree,
Oh, vow to live and die for it, if glorious death must be!
The brave of all the centuries gone this starry Flag have wrought;
In dungeons dim, on gory fields, its light and peace were bought;
And you who front the future—whose days our dreams fulfil—
On Liberty's immortal height, Oh, plant it firmer still!
For it floats for broadest learning; for the soul's supreme release;
For law disdaining license; for righteousness and peace;
For valor born of justice; and its amplest scope and plan
Makes a queen of every woman, a king of every man!
While forever, like Columbus, o'er Truth's unfathomed main
It pilots to the hidden isles, a grander realm to gain.

Ah! what a mighty trust is ours, the noblest ever sung,
To keep this Banner spotless its kindred stars among!
Our fleets may throng the oceans—our forts the headlands crown—
Our mines their treasures lavish for mint and mart and town—
Rich fields and flocks and busy looms bring plenty, far and wide—
And statelier temples deck the land than Rome's or Athens' pride—
And science dare the mysteries of earth and wave and sky—
Till none with us in splendor and strength and skill can vie;
Yet, should we reckon Liberty and Manhood less than these,
And slight the right of the humblest between our circling seas,—
Should we be false to our sacred past, our fathers' God forgetting,
This Banner would lose its lustre, our sun be nigh its setting!
But the dawn will sooner forget the east, the tides their ebb and flow,
Than you forget our radiant Flag, and its matchless gifts forego!
Nay! you will keep it high-advanced with ever-brightening sway—
The Banner whose light betokens the Lord's diviner day—
Leading the nations gloriously in Freedom's holy way!
No cloud on the field of azure—no stain on the rosy bars—
God bless you, Youths and Maidens, as you guard the Stripes and Stars!

EDNA DEAN PROCTOR.

Prepared by The Youth's Companion.

THE ADDRESS FOR COLUMBUS DAY.

"THE MEANING OF THE FOUR CENTURIES."

The spectacle America presents this day is without precedent in history. From ocean to ocean, in city, village, and country-side, the children of the States are marshaled and marching under the banner of the nation: and with them the people are gathering around the schoolhouse.

Men are recognizing to-day the most impressive anniversary since Rome celebrated her thousandth year—the 400th anniversary of the stepping of a hemisphere into the world's life; four completed centuries of a new social order; the celebration of liberty and enlightenment organized into a civilization.

And while, during these hours, the Federal government of these United States strikes the keynote of this great American day that gives honor to the common American institution which unites us all,—we assemble here that we, too, may exalt the free school that embodies the American principle of universal enlightenment and equality: the most characteristic product of the four centuries of American life.

Four hundred years ago this morning the *Pinta's* gun broke the silence, and announced the discovery of this hemisphere.

It was a virgin world. Human life hitherto upon it had been without significance. In the Old World for thousands of years civilized men had been trying experiments in social order. They had been found wanting. But here was an untouched soil that lay ready for a new experiment in civilization. All things were ready. New forces had come to light, full of overturning power in the Old World. In the New World they were to work together with a mighty harmony.

It was for Columbus, propelled by this fresh life, to reveal the land where these new forces were to be given space for development, and where the awaited trial of the new civilization was to be made.

To-day we reach our most memorable milestone. We look backward and we look forward.

Backward, we see the first mustering of modern ideas; their long conflict with Old World theories, which were also transported hither. We see stalwart men and brave women, one moment on the shore, then disappearing in dim forests. We hear the axe. We see the flame of burning cabins and hear the cry of the savage. We see the never-ceasing wagon trains always toiling westward. We behold log cabins becoming villages, then cities. We watch the growth of institutions out of little beginnings—schools becoming an educational system; meeting-houses leading into organic Christianity; town-meetings growing to political movements; county discussions developing federal governments.

We see hardy men with intense convictions, grappling, struggling, often amid battle smoke, and some idea characteristic of the New World always triumphing. We see settlements knitting together into a nation with singleness of purpose. We note the birth of the modern system of industry and commerce, and its striking forth into undreamed-of wealth, making the millions members one of another as sentiment could never bind. And under it all, and through it all, we fasten on certain principles ever operating and regnant—the leadership of manhood; equal rights for every soul; universal enlightenment as the source of progress. These last are the principles that have shaped America; these principles are the true Americanism.

We look forward. We are conscious we are in a period of transition. Ideas in education, in political economy, in social science are undergoing revisions. There is a large uncertainty about the outcome. But faith in the underlying principles of Americanism and in God's destiny for the Republic makes a firm ground of hope. The coming century promises to be more than ever the age of the people; an age that shall develop a greater care for the rights of the weak, and make a more solid provision for the development of each individual by the education that meets his need.

As no prophet among our fathers on the 300th anniversary of America could have pictured what the new century would do, so no man can this day reach out and grasp the hundred years upon which the nation is now entering. On the victorious results of the completed centuries, the principles of Americanism will build our fifth century. Its material progress is beyond our conception, but we may be sure that in the social relations of men with men, the most triumphant gains are to be expected. America's fourth century has been glorious; America's fifth century must be made happy.

One institution more than any other has wrought out the achievements of the past, and is to-day the most trusted for the future. Our fathers in their wisdom knew that the foundations of liberty, fraternity, and equality must be universal education. The free school, therefore, was conceived the corner-stone of the Republic. Washington and Jefferson recognized that the education of citizens is not the prerogative of church or of other private interest; that while religious training belongs to the church, and while technical and higher culture may be given by private institutions—the training of citizens in the common knowledge and the common duties of citizenship belongs irrevocably to the State.

We, therefore, on this anniversary of America present the Public School as the noblest expression of the principle of enlightenment which Columbus grasped by faith. We uplift the system of free and universal education as the master-force which, under God, has been informing each of our generations with the peculiar truths of Americanism. America, therefore, gathers her sons around the schoolhouse to-day as the institution closest to the people, most characteristic of the people, and fullest of hope for the people.

To-day America's fifth century begins. The world's twentieth century will soon be here. To the 13,000,000 now in the American schools the command of the coming years belongs. We, the youth of America, who to-day unite to march as one army under the sacred flag, understand our duty. We pledge ourselves that the flag shall not be stained; and that America shall mean equal opportunity and justice for every citizen, and brotherhood for the world.

HOW TO OBSERVE COLUMBUS DAY.

The Morning Celebration.

The foregoing Official Programme provides for a Morning Celebration. The pupils of the schools are to gather on October 21, at the usual hour, in their respective schoolhouses. As far as possible, all the rooms in each schoolhouse under the same principal should unite in having the same exercises. The parents and friends of the pupils should be brought together. Family interests on Columbus Day should be made to centre in the particular schoolhouse where the children attend.

The exercises of the morning may be simple or elaborate. Schools with sufficient resources may extend the Official Programme with additional features, such as special music by chorus or orchestra, and historical exercises. The largest liberty is left for individual ingenuity and taste.

Afternoon Observances.

In the country, the day ought to be made a real holiday. Farm and household work might be well relinquished; and the families of the district come together at the schoolhouse, with their picnic lunches, prepared to make a day of memorable festivity. Th

The History of the Pledge of Allegiance

"In 1492, Columbus sailed the oceans blue."

That line has been recited by school children in America for years. And school children, for just as many years have recognized Columbus Day as a day commemorating the meeting of two cultures–European and American.

3. SALUTE TO THE FLAG, *by the Pupils.*

At a signal from the Principal the pupils, in ordered ranks, hands to the side, face the Flag. Another signal is given; every pupil gives the Flag the military salute—right hand lifted, palm downward, to a line with the forehead and close to it. Standing thus, all repeat together, slowly: "I pledge allegiance to my Flag and the Republic for which it stands: one Nation indivisible, with Liberty and Justice for all." At the words, "to my Flag," the right hand is extended gracefully, palm upward, towards the Flag, and remains in this gesture till the end of the affirmation; whereupon all hands immediately drop to the side. Then, still standing, as the instruments strike a chord, all will sing AMERICA—"My Country, 'tis of Thee."

When the Boston based magazine, *The Youth's Companion*, published an article to help school children celebrate the 400th anniversary of Columbus' famous landing, they also included a newly written "Pledge of Allegiance," which first appeared in the September 8, 1892, issue of the magazine. Though there has been some debate about who actually wrote the pledge, it was probably cowritten by James B. Upham, head of the circulation department, and Francis Bellamy, coworker. Since the original first appeared in print over a century ago, the Pledge of Allegiance has been changed a little.

I give my hand and heart to my country, one nation, one language, one flag.

During the late 1800s school children recited this salute in the mornings.

I pledge allegiance to my flag and to the Republic for which it stands–one Nation indivisible–with liberty and justice for all.

The version above that first appeared in the September 8, 1892, issue of the Boston-based magazine, *The Youth's Companion.*

I pledge allegiance to the flag ***of the United States of America****, and to the Republic for which it stands–one Nation indivisible–with liberty and justice for all.*

A National Flag Conference was held on June 14, 1923. At that conference the words *of the United States of America* were added to clarify that the flag was the flag of the United States.

I pledge allegiance to the flag of the United States of America, and to the Republic for which it stands, one Nation, ***under God****, indivisible–with liberty and justice for all.*

On June 14, 1954, an act of Congress added the words *under God* to the Pledge of Allegiance.

Name ______________________________

The Vocabulary Builder

I ***pledge allegiance*** to the flag of the United States of America and to the ***Republic*** for which it stands, one Nation under God, ***indivisible*** with ***liberty*** and ***justice*** for all.

Define the words below; then use each word in a sentence.

Pledge: ______________________________

____

____

Allegiance: ______________________________

____

____

Republic: ______________________________

____

____

Indivisible: ______________________________

____

____

Liberty: ______________________________

____

____

Justice: ______________________________

____

____

Name ________________________________

Pledge Crossword

Across

1. one of the cowriters of the Pledge of Allegiance
5. the upper left-hand corner of the flag
7. constitutional form of government
9. larger government unit than a state
11. these two make up the U.S. flag
12. freedom
14. blushing color of stripes
15. *The ______ Companion*
16. gesture of honor

Down

2. loyalty
3. can't be divided
4. _____ Jack
6. "The Star-Spangled ______"
8. process of law
10. pointed flag
13. color of the U.S. flag's canton

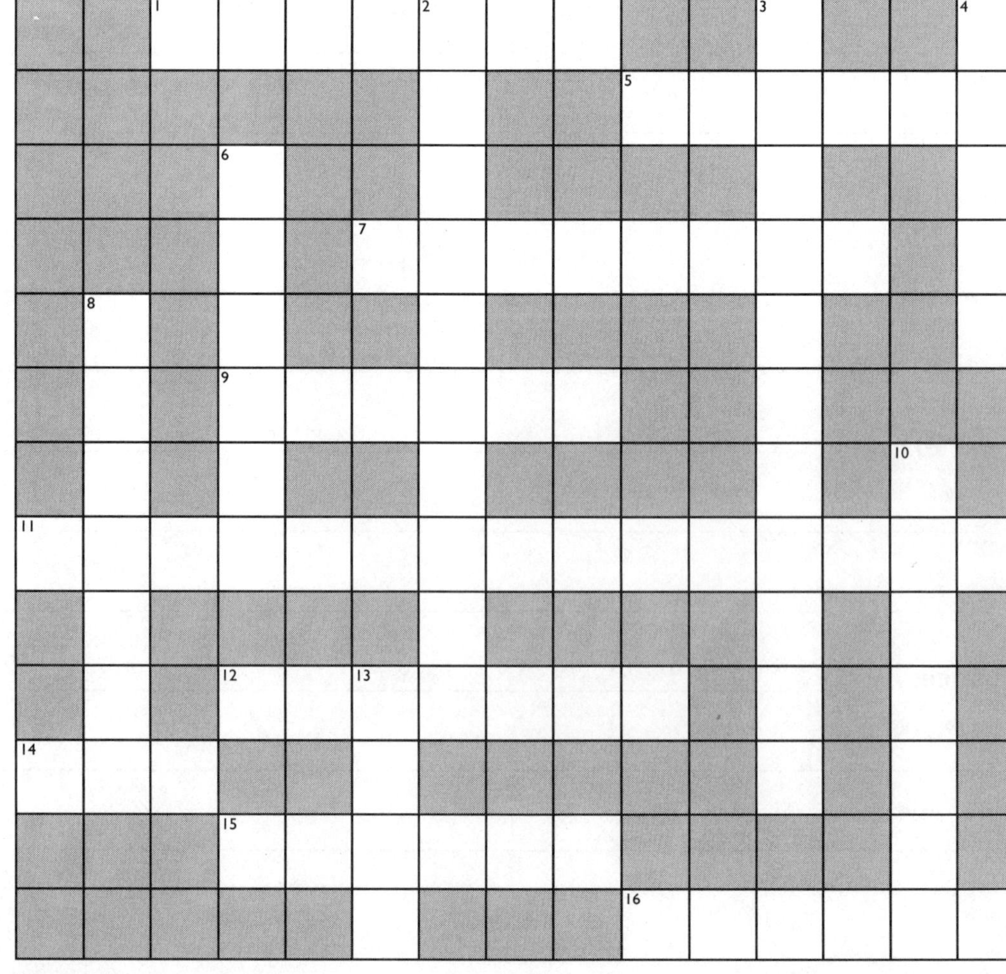

Pledge Flag Comparison

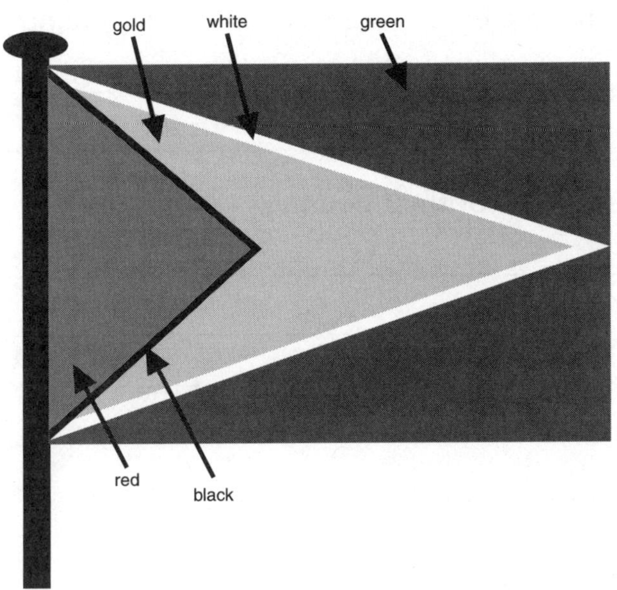

The National Pledge of Guyana

I pledge myself to honour always the Flag of Guyana
and to be loyal to my country
to be obedient to the laws of Guyana
to love my fellow citizens,
and to dedicate my energies towards
the happiness and prosperity of Guyana.

The green in the flag represents agriculture and forests, the white the rivers and water. The gold represents the mineral wealth of Guyana, and the black represents endurance. The red symbolizes the young and independent country dynamically building a nation.

Pledge of Allegiance

I pledge allegiance to the flag
of the United States of America,
and to the Republic
for which it stands,
one Nation under God,
indivisible, with liberty
and justice for all.

Charles Thomson, Secretary of the Continental Congress described, in a report to Congress, that the colors of the Great Seal of the United States, the same colors used in the flag that "white signifies purity and innocence, red, hardiness and valour, and blue, . . . signifies vigilance, perseverance and justice."

Name ___________________________

What's in a Color?

1. Read the National Pledge of Guyana and the description of what the colors of the flag of Guyana represent. Explain how you think the people of Guyana feel about their country.

____

____

2. Do the people of Guyana value the natural resources of their country?

____

____

3. What do the citizens of Guyana pledge to the flag? What do the people of the United States pledge?

____

____

4. How are the statements "obedient to the laws of Guyana" and "justice for all" alike? How are they different?

____

____

5. What does the red, white and blue of the United States' flag represent?

____

____

6. What does the green, white and gold of the flag of Guyana symbolize?

____

____

7. What is the difference between the symbolism of the color of the two flags?

____

____

8. What is the difference between the symbolism of the flags themselves?

____

____

Beyond the Pledge

Find Guyana on a map. On which continent is Guyana located? ____________________

Texas v. Johnson Supreme Court Case 491 U.S. 397 (1989)

Gregory Lee Johnson doused an American flag with kerosene and then lit the flag on fire outside the Dallas, Texas, City Hall while the Republican National Convention was being held in 1984, as fellow protesters shouted, "America, the red, white, and blue, we spit on you." Johnson, who was protesting some of President Ronald Reagan's policies, was arrested and convicted of breaking a Texas state law against desecration of the flag. The case was appealed to the United States Supreme Court, and in June 1989, the court overturned the conviction. Justices Brennan, Marshall, Blackmun, Scalia and Kennedy were in the majority on the court. The majority decision said, in part: "Acknowledging that this Court had not yet decided whether the Government may criminally sanction flag desecration in order to preserve the flag's symbolic value, the Texas court nevertheless concluded that our decision in West Virginia Board of Education v. Barnette . . . suggested that furthering this interest by curtailing speech was impermissible.

"Recognizing that right to differ is the centerpiece of our First Amendment freedoms." The court explained, "a government cannot mandate by fiat a feeling of unity in its citizens. Therefore, that very same government cannot carve out a symbol of unity and prescribe a set of approved messages to be associated with that symbol when it cannot mandate the status or feeling the symbol purports to represent.

" . . . The First Amendment literally forbids the abridgment only of 'speech,' but we have long recognized that its protection does not end at the spoken or written word. While we have rejected 'the view that an apparently limitless variety of conduct can be labeled 'speech' whenever the person engaging in the conduct intends thereby to express an idea' . . . And precisely because it is our flag that is involved, one's response to the burner may exploit the uniquely persuasive power of the flag itself. We can imagine no more appropriate response to burning a flag than waving one's own, no better way to counter a flag burner's message than by saluting the flag that burns, no surer means of preserving the dignity even of the flag that burned than by–as one witness here did–according its remains a respectful burial. We do not consecrate the flag by punishing its desecration, for in doing so we dilute the freedom that this cherished emblem represents."

Chief Justice Rehnquist, and Justices White, O'Connor and Stevens held the minority opinion. "The value of the flag as a symbol cannot be measured. Even so, I have no doubt that the interest in preserving that value for the future is both significant and legitimate. Conceivably that value will be enhanced by the Court's conclusion that our national commitment to prohibit the desecration of its unique symbol. But I am unpersuaded. The creation of a federal right to post bulletin boards and graffiti on the Washington Monument might enlarge the market of free expression, but at a cost I would not pay. Similarly, in my considered judgement, sanctioning the public desecration of the flag will tarnish its value–both for those who cherish the ideas for which it waves and for those who desire to don the robes of martyrdom by burning it. That tarnish is not justified by the trivial burden on free expression occasioned by requiring that an available, alternative mode of expression–including uttering words critical of the flag . . . be employed.

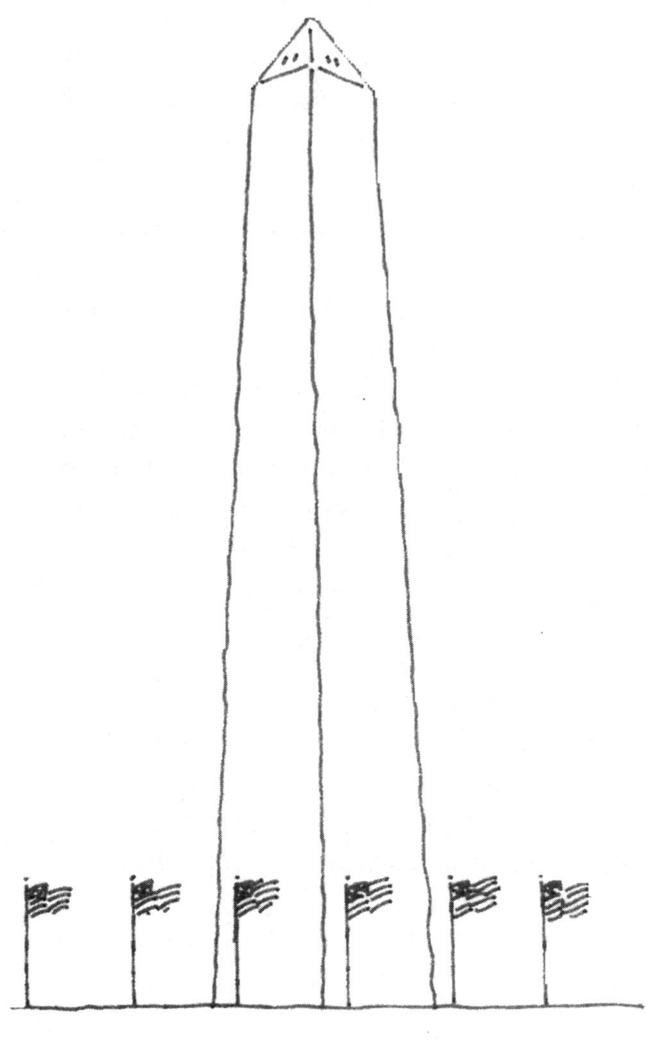

It is appropriate to emphasize certain propositions that are not implicated by this case. The statutory prohibition of flag desecration does not "prescribe what shall be orthodox in politics, nationalism, religion, or other matters of opinion or force citizens to confess by word or act of their faith therein." West Virginia Board of Education v. Barnette, 319 U.S. 624,642 (1943). The statute does not compel any conduct or any profession of respect for any symbol.

The President and the Bill of Rights

Political cartoons are pictorial editorials. That is, the cartoonist sends the message to the reader with a combination of words and pictures. Quite often the cartoonist will use humor, satire and irony to depict his or her point of view.

Caricatures, drawings of people whose features have been exaggerated, are often used in the political cartoons, too. Well-known symbols are used in every form of medium. Some of the best-known symbols are used in advertising. The cartoonist relies on the reader to understand the symbols in the cartoon. Look at this cartoon and answer the questions on the following page.

"But burning the flag goes too far!"

Name ___________________________

The President and the Bill of Rights Cartoon Quiz

1. Who is setting fire to the Bill of Rights in this editorial cartoon?

____

2. How many amendments compromise the Bill of Rights?

____

3. Even though the President is burning all of the amendments in the Bill of Rights, to which amendment, in particular, does the cartoon refer?

____

4. How does the cartoon apply to Texas v. Johnson?

____

____

5. Cartoonist Paul Conrad uses irony to make his point. Describe the use of irony in this cartoon.

____

____

6. Do you consider burning a flag *speech*? Explain your answer.

____

____

Beyond the Cartoon

On the back of this sheet, draw a cartoon that depicts the same point of view as the cartoonist, but use different symbolism.

Flag Burning Draws a Crowd

Political cartoons make their editorial comments through illustration rather than text. Even though most political cartoons contain writing, most of the message is to be found in the art. The cartoonist relies on the reader to understand the message in the cartoon. For this to happen, the reader has to be familiar with the story and the events relating to the cartoon.

Reprinted by permission of Mike Luckovich, Atlanta Constitution, Creators Syndicate © 1989.

Name ______________________________

Flag Burning Draws a Crowd Cartoon Quiz

Study the cartoon and answer the following questions:

1. This cartoon is told in two panels. What does the cartoonist lead you to believe the man in the first panel is talking about when he says, "light one up . . . ."?

____

2. How does the cartoonist, Mike Luckovich, depict the man holding the match?

____

____

3. In the second panel, what is the man setting on fire?

____

4. Describe the expression on the couple's faces looking at the man lighting the flag on fire.

____

5. How does the cartoonist equate cigarette smoking and flag burning?

____

____

6. What is the cartoonist's opinion of flag burning?

____

____

7. Describe the use of humor in the cartoon.

____

____

Beyond the Cartoon

1. On the back of this sheet, draw a cartoon that depicts the same viewpoint using different symbolism.
2. Explain on the back of this sheet why you agree or disagree with the flag burning cartoon?

The Supreme Court and the Pledge of Allegiance

Vocabulary

Jehovah's Witnesses

A religious sect founded by Charles T. Russell, Jehovah's Witnesses take their name from the Bible, Isaiah 43:10 "Ye are my witnesses."

Due Process of Law

Fairly administered arrest and trial, following legal procedures.

First Amendment

Congress shall make no law respecting an establishment of religion, or prohibiting the free exercise thereof; or abridging the freedom of speech, or of the press, or the right of the people peaceably to assemble, and to petition the Government for a redress of grievance.

In 1940, the Supreme Court ruled on a case before them about the Pledge of Allegiance.

Minersville School District v. Gobitis

Mr. Justice Frankfurter delivered the opinion of the Court:

1. Lillian Gobitis, aged twelve, and her brother William, aged ten, were expelled from the public schools of Minersville, Pennsylvania, for refusing to salute the national flag as part of a daily school exercise. The local Board of Education required both teachers and students to participate in this ceremony. The ceremony is a familiar one. The right hand is placed on the breast and the following pledge is recited in unison: "I pledge allegiance to my flag, and to the Republic for which it stands; one nation indivisible, with liberty and justice for all." While the words are spoken teachers and students extend their right hands in salute to the flag. The Gobitis family are affiliated with "Jehovah's Witnesses," for whom the Bible as the Word of God is supreme authority. The children had been brought up conscientiously to believe that such a gesture of respect for the flag was forbidden by command of scripture . . .

2. Centuries of strife over the erection of particular dogmas as exclusive or all comprehending faiths led to the inclusion of a guarantee for religious freedom in the Bill of Rights, the **First Amendment**, and the Fourteenth through its absorption of the First, sought to guard against repetition of those bitter religious struggles by prohibiting the establishment of a state religion and by securing to every sect the free exercise of its faith. So pervasive is the acceptance of this precious right that its scope is brought into question, as here, only when the conscience of individuals collides with the felt necessities of society.

3. We must decide whether the requirement of participation in such a ceremony, exacted from a child who refuses upon sincere religious grounds, infringes without due process of law the liberty guaranteed by the Fourteenth Amendment.

4. In the judicial enforcement of religious freedom, we are concerned with a historic concept. The religious liberty which the Constitution protects has never excluded legislation of general scope not directed against doctrinal loyalties of particular sects. Judicial nullification of legislation cannot be justified by attributing to the framers of the Bill of Rights views for which there is no historic warrant. Conscientious scruples have not, in the course of the long struggle for religious tolerance, relieved the individual from obedience to a general law not aimed at the promotion or restriction of religious beliefs. The mere possession of religious convictions which contradict the relevant concerns of a political society does not relieve the citizen from the discharge of political responsibilities. In all these cases the general laws in question, upheld in their application to those who refused obedience from religious conviction, were manifestations of specific powers of government deemed by the legislation essential to secure and maintain that orderly, tranquil, and free society without religious tolerance itself is unattainable . . .

5. The case before us is not concerned with an exertion of legislative power for the promotion of some specific need or interest of secular society–the protection of the family, the promotion of health, the common defense, the raising of public revenues to defray the cost of government. But all these specific activities of government presuppose the existence of an organized political society. The ultimate foundation of a free society is the binding tie of cohesive sentiment. Such a sentiment is fostered by all those agencies of the mind and spirit which may serve to gather up the traditions of people, transmit them from generation to generation, and thereby create the continuity of treasured common life which constitutes a civilization. We live by symbols. The flag is a symbol of our national unity, transcending all internal differences, however large, within the framework of the Constitution . . .

6. The wisdom of training children in patriotic impulses by those compulsions which necessarily pervade so much of the educational process is not for our independent judgement. Even were we convinced of the folly of such a measure, such belief would be no proof of its unconstitutionality. For ourselves we might be tempted to say that the deepest patriotism is best engendered by giving unfettered scope to the most crotchety beliefs. Perhaps it is best, even from the standpoint of those interests which ordinances like the one under review seek to promote, to give to the least popular sect leave from conformities like those here in issue. But the court-room is not the arena for debating issues of educational policy. It is not our province to choose from competing considerations in the subtle process of effective loyalty to the traditional ideals of democracy, while respecting at the same time individual idiosyncrasies among a people so diversified in racial origins and religious allegiances. So to hold would in effect make us the school board for the country. That authority has not been given to this court, nor should we assume it.

Name ______________________________

Understanding Minersville School District v. Gobitis

1. In paragraph 1 of the court case, explain why Lillian and William Gobitis do not want to salute the flag or recite the Pledge of Allegiance.

____

____

2. In paragraph 2 of the court case, what protects religious freedom?

____

3. What reason is given in paragraph 5 of the decision to compel the Gobitis children to salute the flag and recite the pledge?

____

____

4. In paragraph 6, what reason is stated for not making a decision to strike down making the pledge mandatory?

____

____

Your Opinion

Do you agree with this decision? Why or why not? Explain your answer on the back of this sheet.

The Supreme Court and the Pledge of Allegiance

Vocabulary

Appellees

One against whom an appeal is taken.

Compulsory

Required

Orthodox

Traditional and established beliefs especially referring to religious practices.

In less than three years after the Minersville School District v. Gobitis Case, the Supreme Court rendered another opinion on requiring school children to say the Pledge of Allegiance.

West Virginia State Board of Education v. Barnette

Mr. Justice Jackson delivered the opinion of the Court:

1. . . .The Board of Education adopted a resolution ordering that the salute (and Pledge of Allegiance) to the flag become "a regular part of the program of activities in the public schools," that all teachers and pupils "shall be required to participate in the salute honoring the Nation represented by the flag; provided, however, that refusal to salute the flag be regarded as an act of insubordination, and shall be dealt with accordingly."
2. **Appellees**, citizens of the United States and of West Virginia, brought suit in the United States District Court for themselves and others similarly situated asking an injunction to restrain enforcement of these laws and regulations against Jehovah's Witnesses.
3. The freedom asserted by these appellees does not bring them into collision with rights asserted by any other individual. It is such conflicts which most frequently require intervention of the state to determine where the rights of one end and those of another begin. But the refusal of these persons to participate in the ceremony does not interfere with or deny rights of others to do so. Nor is there any question in this case that their behavior is peaceable and orderly. The sole conflict is between authority and the rights of the individual.
4. There is no doubt that, in connection with the pledges, the flag salute is a form of utterance. Symbolism is a primitive but effective way of communicating ideas. The use of an emblem or flag to symbolize some system, idea, institution, or personality, is a short cut from mind to mind. Causes and nations, political parties, lodges and ecclesiastical groups seek to knit the loyalty of their followings to a flag or banner, a color, or design. The state announces rank, function, and authority through crowns and maces, uniforms and black robes, the church speaks through the Cross, the Crucifix, the alter, and shrine, and clerical raiment. Symbols of state often convey political ideas just as religious symbols come to convey theological ones. Associated with many of these symbols are appropriate gestures of acceptance or respect: a salute, a bowed or bared head, a bended knee. A person gets from a symbol the meaning he puts into it, and what is one man's comfort and inspiration is another's jest and scorn . . .

5. To sustain the **compulsory** flag salute we are required to say that a Bill of Rights which guards the individual's right to speak his own mind, left it open to public authorities to compel him to utter what is not in his mind . . .

6. The case is made difficult not because the principles of its decision are obscure but because the flag involved is our own. Nevertheless, we apply the limitations of the Constitution with no fear that freedom to be intellectually and spiritually diverse or even contrary will disintegrate the social organization. To believe that patriotism will not flourish if patriotic ceremonies are voluntary and spontaneous instead of a compulsory routine is to make an unflattering estimate of the appeal of our institutions to free minds. We can have intellectual individualism and the rich cultural diversities that owe to exceptional minds only at the price of occasional eccentricity and abnormal attitudes. When they are so harmless to others or the State as those we deal with here, the price is not too great. But freedom to differ is not limited to things that so not matter much. That would be a mere shadow of freedom. The test of its substance is the right to differ as to things that touch the heart of the existing order . . .
7. If there is any fixed star in our constitutional constellation, it is that no official, high or petty, can prescribe what shall be **orthodox** in politics, nationalism, religion, or other matters of opinion or force citizens to confess by word or act their faith therein. If there are any circumstances which permit exception, they do not occur to us.
8. We think the action of the local authorities in compelling the flag salute and pledge transcends constitutional limitations on their power and invades the sphere of intellect and spirit it is the purpose of the First Amendment to our Constitution to reserve from all official control . . .

Understanding West Virginia State Board of Education v. Barnette

1. Why did the appellees bring this case to court (paragraph 2)?

2. Read paragraph 4 and describe how the decision defines a symbol. What is the symbol in this case?

3. Why is a compulsory flag salute at odds with the Bill of Rights? Which amendment protects freedom of speech?

4. Why is this case in particular a difficult case to decide?

5. What is the decision?

Your Opinion

Do you agree with this decision? Explain your answer on the back of this sheet.

Beyond the Decision

Compare this decision to the decision made in Texas v. Johnson, 1989. What are the issues that concerned the cases?

Bibliography

Resources for Teachers

Eggenberger, David. *Flags of the U.S.A.: An Illustrated History of the Stars and Stripes from Its Beginnings to the 50th Star.* New York: Thomas Y. Crowell Company, 1964.

Guenter, Scot. *The American Flag 1777-1924: Cultural Shifts from Creation to Codification.* London and Toronto: Fairleigh Dickinson University Press, 1990.

Morris, Robert. *The Truth About the American Flag.* Beach Haven, New Jersey: Wynnehaven Publishing Co., 1976.

Pfeffer, Leo. *Religious Freedom.* Lincolnwood, Illinois: National Textbook Company, 1977.

Quaife, Milo Milton. *The Flag of the United States.* New York: Grosset & Dunlap, 1942.

Suggested Books for Students

Richtel, Anne Miller. *Murray's Salute to the Flag.* Fresno, California, 1987.

Swanson, June. *I Pledge Allegiance.* Minneapolis, Minnesota: Carolrhoda Books Inc., 1990.

Williams, Jr., Earl P. *What You Should Know About the American Flag.* Gettysburg, Pennsylvania: Thomas Publications, 1992.

Answer Key

Flag Match, page 11

1. d, 2. c, 3. g, 4. a, 5. b, 6. h, 7. f, 8. e

Parts of the Flag, page 12

1. d, 2. e, 3. a, 4. g, 5. f, 6. c, 7. b

Pledge Crossword, page 16

Across	Down
1. Bellamy	2. allegiance
5. canton	3. indivisible
7. Republic	4. Union
9. nation	6. Banner
11. Stars and Stripes	8. justice
12. liberty	10. pennant
14. red	13. blue
15. Youth's	
16. salute	

What's in a Color? page 18

1. Answers will vary. However, the colors in the flag represent the rivers, the forests and the mineral riches of the country. It would seem that the people of Guyana love their land and country a great deal to have the colors in their national symbol represent their land and forests.
2. Answers will vary.
3. The citizens of Guyana pledge to honor; the citizens of the United States pledge allegiance.
4. Answers will vary. Both indicate a respect for laws, *obedience* indicates that the person will be law abiding–*justice for all* is a wish that the laws of the country will be just for everyone. One is a promise to obey; one is a promise for a higher principle–justice.
5. **white**–purity and innocence; **red**–hardiness and valor; **blue**–vigilance, perseverance and justice
6. **green**–agriculture and forests; **white**–rivers; **gold**–mineral wealth; **black**–endurance
7. Answers will vary. For the most part, the colors in the U.S. flag represent abstract concepts, lofty qualities such as valor, justice, etc. The colors of the flag of Guyana represent concrete things such as rivers, minerals, agriculture, forests–the exception is the color black in the flag, which represents endurance.
8. The symbols that make up the flag of Guyana represent large items such as rivers, agriculture, etc. The U.S. flag, on the other hand, is made of symbols that represent very concrete units of government. Stars represent states; the stripes represent the original 13 colonies.

Beyond the Pledge, page 18

South America

The President and the Bill of Rights Cartoon Quiz, page 22

1. President George Bush
2. 10
3. First Amendment
4. The First Amendment protects freedom of speech. The Supreme Court ruled burning a flag is symbolic speech, therefore is protected.
5. The irony of the cartoon is that while George Bush protests about burning the flag, according to the cartoonist, he is willing to set the First Amendment on fire to protect the flag from flag burners.
6. Answers will vary.

Flag Burning Draws a Crowd Cartoon Quiz, page 24

1. lighting up a cigarette
2. He is balding, overweight and sloppy
3. U.S. flag
4. horrified
5. Cigarette smoking, though legal, is unhealthy. People stare and glare at smokers, who are often forced to smoke outside. Flag burning, though legal, is also frowned upon by many.
6. against it
7. This cartoon pokes fun at smokers and flag burners.

Understanding Minersville School District v. Gobitis, page 27

1. because it is against their religion
2. First Amendment
3. The ultimate foundation of a free society is the binding tie of cohesive sentiment–fostered by all those agencies of the mind and spirit which may serve to gather up the traditions of people, transmit them from generation to generation, and thereby create the continuity of treasured common life which constitutes a civilization.
4. The Supreme Court does not want to rule on what is best for school children. The Court says that decision is up to local school boards.

Understanding West Virginia State Board of Education v. Barnette, page 30

1. on behalf of the Jehovah's Witnesses
2. "A primitive but effective way of communicating ideas"–the United States flag
3. Our Constitution was written so that "no official, high or petty, can prescribe what shall be orthodox, in politics, nationalism, religion, or other matters of opinion . . ."–First Amendment
4. Because the United States flag, a symbol dear to our country, is involved.
5. That no one should be forced to recite the pledge against their will.